Al Capone Does My Shirts
Lit Link

Grades 4-6

Written by Nat Reed
Illustrated by Tom Goldsmith

About the author: Nat Reed has been a member of the teaching profession for over 30 years. He is presently a full-time instructor at Trent University in the Teacher Education Program.

ISBN 978-1-55035-892-6
Copyright 2007
All Rights Reserved * Printed in Canada

Permission to Reproduce

Permission is granted to the individual teacher who purchases one copy of this book to reproduce the student activity material for use in his/her classroom only. Reproduction of these materials for an entire school or for a school system, or for other colleagues or for commercial sale is **strictly prohibited**. No part of this publication may be transmitted in any form or by any means, electronic, mechanical, recording or otherwise without the prior written permission of the publisher. "We acknowledge the financial support of the Government of Canada through the Book Publishing Industry Development Program (BPIDP) for this project."

Published in the United States by:
On The Mark Press
3909 Witmer Road PMB 175
Niagara Falls, New York
14305
www.onthemarkpress.com

Published in Canada by:
S&S Learning Materials
15 Dairy Avenue
Napanee, Ontario
K7R 1M4
www.sslearning.com

At A Glance

Learning Expectations	Chapters 1-2	Chapters 3-4	Chapters 5-6	Chapters 7-9	Chapters 10-12	Chapters 13-15	Chapters 16-18	Chapters 19-20	Chapters 21-23	Chapters 24-26	Chapters 27-29	Chapters 30-32	Chapters 33-34	Chapters 35-37	Chapters 38-40
Reading Comprehension															
• Identify and describe story elements	•	•	•	•	•	•	•	•	•	•	•	•	•	•	•
• Summarize events/details	•	•	•	•	•	•	•	•	•	•	•	•	•	•	•
Reasoning & Critical Thinking Skills															
• Identify character traits and make comparisons	•	•		•			•	•						•	
• Use context clues – identify analogies			•			•				•					
• Make inferences (i.e., why events occurred, characters' thoughts and feelings, etc.)	•	•			•		•	•		•	•	•			•
• Determine the meaning of colloquialisms and other phrases		•	•		•			•							•
• Understand abstract concepts – conscience, revenge, fear, perseverance, self-respect, exaggeration, conflict, etc.	•	•	•	•	•	•	•	•	•	•	•	•	•	•	•
• Develop opinions and personal interpretations	•	•	•		•	•	•	•	•			•	•	•	
• Write a letter/editorial for a newspaper							•				•				
• Conduct an interview										•					
• Develop research skills	•	•			•										
• Develop a poster or book cover												•			•
• Identify conflict						•						•			
• Identify setting	•														
• Create a time line															•
• Identify cliffhangers and foreshadowing					•				•			•			
Language Skills															
• Identify synonyms, antonyms, and homonyms			•						•	•		•	•		
• Identify similes	•				•									•	
• Identify literary devices: personification, exaggeration, sarcasm, onomatopoeia	•					•				•		•			
• Identify syllables			•												
• Identify compound words														•	
• Identify descriptive words and phrases	•	•													
• Identify parts of speech									•	•					
• Dictionary and thesaurus skills		•		•	•		•		•		•	•	•	•
• Use words correctly in sentences	•						•	•							
• Place words in alphabetical order				•											
• Identify singular/plural				•											
• Use capitals and punctuation correctly					•										

Al Capone Does My Shirts
by Gennifer Choldenko

Table of Contents

At A Glance 2

Overall Expectations... 4

List of Activities 5

Teacher Suggestions 6

Synopsis/Author Biography 7

Student Checklist... 8

Reproducible Student Booklet 9

Answer Key.. 59

Al Capone Does My Shirts
by Gennifer Choldenko

Overall Expectations

The students will:

- develop their skills in reading, writing, listening, and oral communication

- use good literature as a vehicle for developing skills required by curriculum expectations: reasoning and critical thinking, knowledge of language structure, vocabulary building, and use of conventions

- become meaningfully engaged in the drama of literature through a variety of types of questions and activities

- identify and describe elements of stories (i.e., plot, main idea, characters, setting)

- learn and review many skills in order to develop good reading habits

- provide clear answers to questions and well-constructed explanations

- organize and classify information to clarify thinking

- learn about autism as a learning exceptionality, the North American penal system, responsibility, family dynamics, and societal stereotyping

- relate events and feelings found in novels to their own lives and experiences

- appreciate the importance of friendship and loyalty in personal relationships

- appreciate the role and responsibilities of parents and authoritative figures in the lives of young people

- learn the importance of dealing with adversity and developing perseverance in the face of adversity

- state their own interpretation of a written work, using evidence from the work and from their own knowledge and experience

Al Capone Does My Shirts
by Gennifer Choldenko

List of Skills

Vocabulary Development:

1. Identifying/creating similes
2. Locating descriptive words/phrases
3. Listing synonyms, antonyms, homonyms
4. Using capitals and punctuation
5. Identifying syllables
6. Listing compound words
7. Identifying sarcasm
8. Using singular/plural nouns
9. Using context clues: analogies
10. Identifying parts of speech
11. Determining alphabetical order
12. Identifying onomatopoeia
13. Identifying root words
14. Identifying exaggeration

Setting Activities:

1. Summarizing the details of a setting
2. Creating a time chart

Plot Activities:

1. Completing a time line of events
2. Identifying foreshadowing
3. Determining the role of others in one's personal growth
4. Identifying conflict in the story
5. Identifying cliffhangers

Character Activities:

1. Determining character traits
2. Comparing two characters
3. Understanding concepts such as perseverance, self respect, stereotypes, responsibility
4. Relating personal experiences

Creative and Critical Thinking:

1. Researching historical figures
2. Writing an editorial on an issue
3. Writing a letter to a friend
4. Conducting an interview
5. Writing a description of personal feelings

Art Activities:

1. Designing a poster
2. Designing a cover for the novel

Al Capone Does My Shirts
by Gennifer Choldenko

Teacher Suggestions

This resource can be used in a variety of ways:

1. The student booklet focuses on one chapter of the novel at a time. Each of these sections contains the following activities:

   a) **Before you read the chapters** (reasoning and critical thinking skills)
   b) **Vocabulary building** (dictionary and thesaurus skills)
   c) **Questions on the chapter** (reading comprehension skills)
   d) **Language activities** (grammar, punctuation, word structure, and extension activities)

2. Students may read the novel at their own speed and then select, or be assigned, a variety of questions and activities.

3. **Bulletin Board and Interest Center Ideas:** themes might include the 1930s (Great Depression, baseball stars), prisons (esp. Alcatraz), California, gangsters of the 1930s.

4. **Pre-Reading Activities:** *Al Capone Does My Shirts* may also be used in conjunction with themes of acceptance of people with exceptionalities or learning disabilities, autism, self-esteem, perseverance, family values, societal prejudice, the danger of placing too much emphasis on social status, the North American penal system in the 1930s compared to today.

5. **Independent Reading Approach:** Students who are able to work independently may attempt to complete the assignments in a self-directed manner. Initially these students should participate in the pre-reading activities with the rest of the class. Students should familiarize themselves with the reproducible student booklet. Completed worksheets should be submitted so that the teacher can note how quickly and accurately the students are working. Students may be brought together periodically to discuss issues in specific sections of the novel.

6. **Fine Art Activities:** students may integrate such topics as California, prisons, life in the 1930s (e.g., technology, sports, forms of entertainment, education).

7. Encourage the students to keep a reading log in which they record their readings each day and their thoughts about the passage.

8. Students should keep all their work together in one place. A portfolio cover is provided for this reason.

9. Students should not be expected to complete all activities. Teachers should allow choice and in some cases match the activity to the student's ability.

10. Students should keep track (in their portfolio) of the activities they complete.

Al Capone Does My Shirts

by Gennifer Choldenko

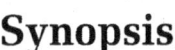

Synopsis

It is 1935 and Moose Flanagan's dad has just been hired to work as an electrician on Alcatraz Island, home to the most famous prison in the United States. What is worse, Moose's whole family is moving to the island to take up residence next door to Al Capone, Machine Gun Kelly, and a host of other notorious convicts.

Complicating an already dicey situation is Moose's autistic sister, Natalie, whom the family is trying desperately to have enrolled in the Esther P. Marinoff School.

A number of other children live on the island; children whose parents live and work at the prison. Among these is Piper, the precocious daughter of the warden. Although Moose finds himself attracted to Piper, her wild, money-making schemes are constantly landing her in trouble with the prison authorities.

Moose is troubled by his mother's growing obsession with having Natalie admitted into the Marinoff school. As a result, Moose is given more and more responsibility in looking after his sister, and helping her to be accepted by his friends. When the school rejects Natalie for the second time, Moose writes Al Capone a letter to see if the famous gangster can pull a few strings to help the family out. He does!

Perhaps the novel's greatest contribution is providing the young reader with a better understanding of autism, and the stress it can bring to bear upon families. The novel also provides a revealing window into family dynamics and the interplay between parent and child during stressful times.

Author Biography

Gennifer Choldenko

Gennifer Choldenko was born in Santa Monica, California – not far from the setting of *Al Capone Does My Shirts*. She was the youngest of four children. Gennifer knew that she wanted to be a writer when she was only six years old.

Choldenko majored in literature and creative writing at Brandeis University, then after graduation entered the world of advertising (which she grew to hate). She then attended the Rhode Island School of Design where she received a degree in illustration.

Gennifer's first published book was the picture book, *Moonstruck: The True Story of the Cow Who Jumped Over the Moon*, published by Hyperion. Since then she has seen her novels, *Notes From a Liar and Her Dog*, *A Tree Falls at Lunch Period*, *How to Make Friends With a Giant*, and Newbery Honor Book *Al Capone Does My Shirts* also published. She chose Alcatraz as the setting for *Al Capone Does My Shirts* after reading a San Francisco Chronicle article about the prison guards' children who grew up on The Rock.

Gennifer has two terrific kids: a son, Ian, age 12, and a daughter, Kai, age 7, and lives in the San Francisco Bay area.

Al Capone Does My Shirts
by Gennifer Choldenko

Student Checklist

Student Name: _____

Assignment	Grade/Level	Comments

Al Capone Does My Shirts
by Gennifer Choldenko

Name:_____

Al Capone Does My Shirts

by Gennifer Choldenko

Chapters 1 – 2

Before you read the chapters:

Al Capone Does My Shirts has a very unique setting: Alcatraz Prison. What would be two other unusual places for a kid to grow up?

_____
_____
_____

Vocabulary:

Choose a word from the list to complete each sentence.

| smithereens | felon | circuits | embezzler | tantrums |
| buoy | stilts | apparent | picky | affliction |

1. An _____ is usually a person who steals funds from the company he or she works for.

2. My sister is a very _____ eater.

3. It was very _____ that someone had spilled mustard on the carpet.

4. The car was smashed to _____ at the crash-up derby.

5. The speedboat accidentally ran over the _____ close to the beach.

6. By using a pair of _____ he was able to see over the fence and into the ballpark.

7. His uncle, Jack, is a convicted _____, who spent time in Alcatraz.

8. All of the electrical _____ in the old house needed replacing.

9. A case of measles was the latest _____ that my little sister had to endure.

10. By the time he was four years old, he had finally stopped having temper _____.

Al Capone Does My Shirts

by Gennifer Choldenko

Questions:

1. a) Reread the first paragraph of Chapter 1. What question comes to mind when you read this paragraph?

   b) With what impression of Alcatraz does this paragraph leave you?

   c) The setting of a story includes not only the place (Alcatraz Island in this novel), but also the time. When did this story take place?

2. How did Moose and Natalie come to live on Alcatraz Island?

3. What do you think Moose means when he says that the kids at Esther P. Marinoff School have macaroni salad in their hair and wear their clothes inside out?

4. Why didn't the guards at Alcatraz, except for those stationed high in the towers or catwalks, carry guns?

5. What is unusual about Natalie?

6. When Moose talks about how he got his nickname, what do you think he means by saying, "I started growing to fit the name that very day"?

Al Capone Does My Shirts
by Gennifer Choldenko

7. What precautions did Moose take on his first night at Alcatraz? Do you think these precautions were necessary? Explain your answer.
   _____
   _____

8. Briefly describe Theresa Mattaman. Be sure to include her personality as well as her general appearance.
   _____
   _____
   _____

Language Activities:

1. Eleanor Roosevelt is mentioned in Chapter 2. Who was this woman? List one of her many accomplishments.
   _____
   _____
   _____

2. The author enjoys using **similes** in this novel. A simile is a comparison between two things using the words **like** or **as**. An example is found in Chapter 1: "there's water all around, black and shiny like tar."

   In this example, **water** is compared to _____.

   Use **similes** to compare the following:

   a) A vegetable to an iceberg: _____

   b) Thunder to (your choice): _____

   c) The surface of a lake to (your choice): _____

3. Another literary device the author enjoys using is **exaggeration**. An example of this is found in the following description: "it sounds like dozens of mice are dying an ugly death." Find another example of exaggeration from the first two chapters.
   _____
   _____

Al Capone Does My Shirts
by Gennifer Choldenko

4. Natalie's father calls her "sweet pea" at one point in Chapter 2. This is known as a **term of endearment**. Come up with three other popular terms of endearment.

_____
_____
_____

5. Research several interesting facts about one of the following gangsters from the 1930s: Machine Gun Kelly, Baby Face Nelson, Al Capone, Roy Gardner, Doc Barker, John Dillinger, or Pretty Boy Floyd. Be sure to include whether or not they were ever prisoners at Alcatraz. Print a picture of your gangster off the Internet and paste it onto your profile.

File # 020202

Photo

Name: _____

Al Capone Does My Shirts

by Gennifer Choldenko

Chapters 3 – 4

Before you read the chapters:

Meeting new people is often difficult, especially when you move to a new neighborhood. In these next two chapters, Moose meets a very interesting girl named Piper who provides some interesting challenges for Moose. From your own experiences, describe a personal incident in which you met someone with whom you found it very difficult to strike up a friendship. What was there about this person that made it difficult for you?

_____
_____
_____

Vocabulary:

Using the words from the Word Box, complete the following crossword puzzle.

Capone	Moose	Piper	Alcatraz	Natalie	autistic	fake
peculiar	cleat	pronounce	beet	realize	snitch	scowl
aches	resume	swipe	out	one	entered	armed
rests	able	rm	suddenly	haste	ice	ate

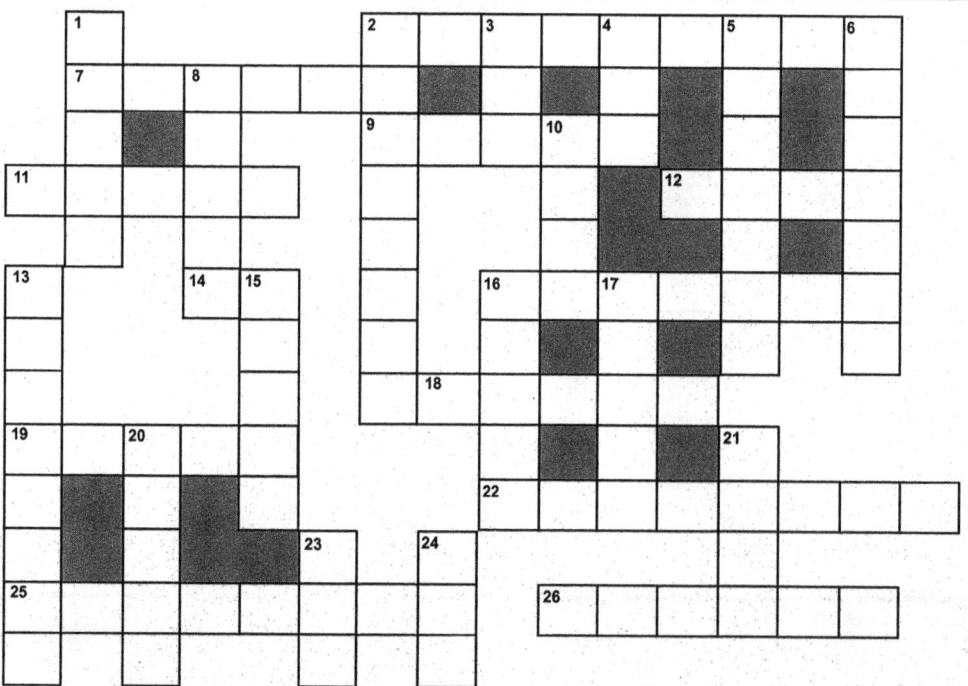

Al Capone Does My Shirts
by Gennifer Choldenko

Down

1. A look of anger
2. Odd
3. A small number
4. Not in
5. Moose's sister
6. Gone into
8. The warden's daughter
10. Capable
13. A famous prison
15. The novel's main character
16. Relaxes
17. Having a gun on one's person
20. Hurry
21. A red vegetable
23. He ___ a sandwich.
24. Used to keep drinks cool

Across

2. To say clearly
7. The most famous convict in Alcatraz
9. Piece of metal on the sole of a shoe
11. Slang for to steal
12. Not genuine
14. Short for revolutions/minute
16. To understand
18. To begin again
19. Pains
22. All at once
25. Having a kind of learning exceptionality
26. Someone who tattles on someone else

Questions:

1. What job had Piper assigned to Theresa?

2. How many boys were on Alcatraz Island?

3. a) What were Al Capone's nicknames?

   b) If Al Capone was still alive today, how old would he be?

4. What do you think the term **gangster amnesia** means? Why might a person contract this affliction?

Al Capone Does My Shirts
by Gennifer Choldenko

5. Why weren't Bonnie and Clyde at Alcatraz?
   _____
   _____

6. Why do you think it upsets Moose so much when someone asks about what's wrong with Natalie?
   _____
   _____

7. What unusual ability did Natalie have?
   _____
   _____

8. What did Moose mean when he said, "How am I supposed to know if Nat's a big secret or not"?
   _____
   _____

9. Do you agree with Moose when he says that you can't fake being pleased to see someone? Explain your answer.
   _____
   _____

10. What is a "snitch box"?
    _____
    _____

11. Describe why it was such an upsetting experience for Moose when they took Natalie to her boarding school.
    _____
    _____

Al Capone Does My Shirts

by Gennifer Choldenko

Language Activities:

1. Investigate **autism**. Describe two or three interesting characteristics of people who are autistic. Describe their strengths and areas where they experience difficulty. Do you know anyone who is autistic?

   _____
   _____
   _____
   _____

2. Research two interesting facts about the item in the book *The American Leaf-Nosed Bat* that caught Natalie's attention.

   _____
   _____
   _____
   _____

3. The author enjoys including unusual expressions in this novel. Put the following expressions in your own words:

   a) Make a beeline there.

   _____
   _____

   b) Twelve minutes to get to Alcatraz, twenty years to get back.

   _____
   _____

   c) Natalie lives in her own world.

   _____
   _____

Al Capone Does My Shirts

by Gennifer Choldenko

Chapters 5 – 6

Before you read the chapters:

Being taken advantage of by someone else is usually not a pleasant experience. Tell about a personal experience or an experience that happened to someone you know, when this occurred.

_____
_____
_____

Describe how it made you feel.

_____
_____

Vocabulary:

In each of the following sets of words, underline the one word that does not belong. Then write a sentence explaining why it does not fit.

1. asylum   hospice   institution   obsession
   _____

2. ashen   pail   pale   blanch
   _____

3. cowardly   humane   kind   civilized
   _____

4. impressive   ferocious   awe-inspiring   moving
   _____

5. mute   silent   quiet   menacing
   _____

Al Capone Does My Shirts

by Gennifer Choldenko

6. deliberate   grisly   ghastly   appalling

_____

7. precisely   accurately   grossly   exactly

_____

Questions:

Complete the following exercise filling in the correct words from the Word Box.

limelight	terrible	outsiders	library	guard
convicts	Piper	projects	exception	contact
time	warden	Natalie	asylum	understand

Mrs. McCraw offended Moose's mom by saying that Natalie belonged in an _____. When they returned home from taking Natalie to her school, there was a note asking that Moose see the _____ later that afternoon. Moose thought that being a prison _____ was the wrong job for his dad. Moose learned at an early age that getting mad at _____ would never be forgiven. Moose's dad said about _____ that, "the pretty ones are always trouble". Moose's dad said that the _____ darned socks a lot better than his mom.

Moose met the warden in the _____. The warden told him that everyone on Alcatraz must follow the rules without _____. The warden reminded Moose that the convicts were _____ men with nothing but _____ on their hands. The warden thought it important that he and Moose _____ each other. Rule number one: There's no _____ with the convicts. Rule number four: Do not speak to _____ about what goes on here. He said that the point

Al Capone Does My Shirts

by Gennifer Choldenko

of the prison is to keep showy criminals out of the _____. Finally, the warden asked Moose if would mind helping Piper carry her _____ to school.

Language Activities:

1. Put the following expressions from these chapters into your own words:

   Wild-goose chases: _____
   _____

   Cut your losses: _____
   _____

   No use throwing the good after bad: _____
   _____

   A cheap shot: _____
   _____

   All spooky quiet: _____
   _____

2. Choose 10 words from these chapters with two or more **syllables**. Indicate the syllables by drawing a line between each syllable.

   Example: any/where

   _____   _____
   _____   _____
   _____   _____
   _____   _____
   _____   _____

Al Capone Does My Shirts
by Gennifer Choldenko

Chapters 7 – 9

Before you read the chapters:

Either from your own personal experience, or from your imagination, describe how it feels for a new student on the first day of school.
_____
_____

There is an old saying, "You never get a second chance to make a first impression". Come up with a couple of suggestions for making a good first impression when you are meeting new people, as Moose is doing in these chapters.
_____
_____

Vocabulary:

Draw a straight line to connect the vocabulary word to its definition. Remember to use a straight edge (like a ruler).

1.	counterfeit	a)	patio
2.	combination	b)	fidgety
3.	antsy	c)	imitation
4.	arc	d)	invention
5.	earnest	e)	sincere
6.	terrace	f)	praise
7.	elaborate	g)	complicated
8.	contraption	h)	curve
9.	compliment	i)	cutting (referring to words)
10.	sarcastic	j)	things put together

Al Capone Does My Shirts
by Gennifer Choldenko

Questions:

1. What do you think Moose's description of Piper in the opening paragraph tells us about his regard for her?

2. Explain Moose's comment, "Sometimes it seems easier to be Natalie. People force her to do stuff. I have to force myself".

3. In your own words describe Moose's teacher, Miss Bimp. Do you think her name is appropriate? Explain your answer.

4. Why does Moose think it is significant that Piper is the only girl in the class who isn't wearing an apron?

5. Why do you think Moose starts to tell the other students about his life on Alcatraz?

6. We really start to find out what a sense of humor (and imagination) Moose has in these chapters. Find an example of his sense of humor that you particularly enjoyed.

7. Describe Moose's first at bat when playing with the guys after school.

Al Capone Does My Shirts
by Gennifer Choldenko

8. Why do you think he enjoyed playing ball so much?
   _____
   _____

9. Why is Piper upset with Moose in Chapter 9?
   _____
   _____

10. How do you know that Moose secretly likes Piper?
    _____
    _____

Language Activities:

Write the plural of the following nouns from this chapter. Careful - you may wish to consult a dictionary for some of these words.

Singular Noun	Plural Noun
Self	
Speech	
Woman	
Contraption	
Catch	
Cry	
Half	
Church	
Laundry	
Notebook	

Al Capone Does My Shirts
by Gennifer Choldenko

Chapters 10 – 12

Before you read the chapters:

"Consider the postage stamp: its usefulness consists in the ability to stick to one thing till it gets there." ~Josh Billings

In the next few chapters, Moose's family have to endure another setback with regards to Natalie. Consider the above quotation from Josh Billings. How would this be an encouragement to Moose's family in this situation?

_____
_____
_____

When we are young, it is often difficult to understand when adults disappoint us. Why do you think this is true?

_____
_____
_____

Vocabulary:

Choose a word from the list that means the same or nearly the same as the underlined word.

| replicate | swiveled | radiant | adjustment | register |
| permanent | formula | flexibility | diagnosis | sensitive |

1. The gymnast demonstrated great **elasticity** on the parallel bars. _____

2. Did you remember to **sign in** when you arrived? _____

3. The bride was simply **glowing** in her long white gown. _____

4. Moose has a very **tender** heart when it comes to his sister. _____

5. The doctor's **analysis** of her condition was most thorough. _____

Al Capone Does My Shirts

by Gennifer Choldenko

6. "Do you know the **rule** for success?" he asked. _____

7. The inventor was forced to make a slight **modification**. _____

8. Are you trying to **copy** her hair style? _____

9. The warden **turned** in his chair and faced Moose. _____

10. The scar was a **lasting** reminder of his accident. _____

Questions:

1. What disturbing news did Mr. Purdy deliver to Moose?
   _____
   _____

2. Why does Moose tell his dad before telling his mom the news?
   _____
   _____

3. Why did Moose's mom volunteer to go and get Natalie and leave his dad at home?
   _____
   _____

4. Investigate: What do the initials **UCLA** stand for?
   _____

5. Why did Moose find UCLA's involvement with Natalie so upsetting?
   _____
   _____

6. Why did Moose's mom like the program at Purdy's school?
   _____
   _____

Al Capone Does My Shirts

by Gennifer Choldenko

7. Besides her work with UCLA and Purdy's School, name two other ways that Moose's mom tried to help Natalie.

8. What reason did Mr. Purdy give for giving up on Natalie?

9. Do you think Purdy was copping out? Defend your answer.

10. What are "jailhouse lawyers"?

11. What finally changed Moose's mind about helping Piper?

Language Activities:

1. The study of Natalie at UCLA tested her reaction to the composer, Tchaikovsky. Investigate this great musician and come up with three interesting facts about his life and works.

2. Place the following words from this chapter in alphabetical order.

Caconi	can	come	cracks	creases
cereal	child	classroom	children	country

Al Capone Does My Shirts
by Gennifer Choldenko

Chapters 13 – 15

Before you read the chapters:

The assigning of responsibilities by parents to their children has advantages and disadvantages. From your own experience, think of one advantage and one disadvantage to having responsibilities when you're young. You might also consider Moose's situation when answering.

_____
_____
_____
_____

Vocabulary:

Solve the following word search puzzle using the words from the Word Box. Remember – the words can be horizontal, vertical or diagonal. They may be forward or even backward!

| corduroys | natters | precious | wheedle | responsibility | Capone | |
| redirect | victory | gravelly | entertain | revving | huddle | recreation |

```
c a p o n e q w e e l d d u h
e o r t y u i o o p a s d f p
f g r h j y l l e v a r g r e
z x n d c v b n m q w e e v n
q w a e u r t y u i o c r i t
r q t s d r f g h j i r j c e
e a t s c a o s d o f e h t r
d z e z x u y y u t r v e o t
i x r c v b n s s m q v w r a
r e s p o n s i b i l i t y i
e p o u y t r e w q w n d f n
c s d f e l d e e h w g g h j
t s r e c r e a t i o n f g h
```

Al Capone Does My Shirts
by Gennifer Choldenko

Questions:

1. Mrs. Kelly, who is mentioned in Chapter 11, plays an important role in these chapters. What had Mr. Purdy promised Moose's mom in this regard?

2. At the beginning of Chapter 13, what does Moose say to Piper that he immediately regrets? Why?

3. What is your opinion of Mrs. Kelly's advice regarding Natalie? Do you think it is wise advise? Explain your answer.

4. What does Moose's mother want him to start doing? Why is this a serious problem for Moose?

5. After reading Chapter 13, explain why you think the author gave the chapter this particular title.

6. Describe the result of Moose's talk with Scout about changing the time of the ball game.

7. Why did Natalie have a problem understanding Moose's objection to her wearing a bathing suit?

Al Capone Does My Shirts

by Gennifer Choldenko

8. Where do you think Piper got the key to the lock?

Language Activities:

1. Chapter 15 ends on a very suspenseful note (a **cliffhanger**). Use your imagination and briefly predict what you think will happen to Piper and the others.

2. Rewrite the following sentences putting in the correct **capitalization** and **punctuation**.

   a) it was tuesday before moose even got to leave alcatraz

   b) don't you really care what happened to natalie

   c) piper spotted al capone doing laundry at the shady rest hotel

3. **Onomatopoeia** is a literary device **using sound words** "like bang". This literary device is used in Chapter 15 when Piper imitates the sound of a chicken, "bwahk, bwahk, bwahk". Come up with three more examples of this literary device. (They don't have to be from the novel.)

Al Capone Does My Shirts
by Gennifer Choldenko

Chapters 16 – 18

Before you read the chapters:

How important do you think it is that a parent be fair when dealing with their children? Explain your answer with two examples.

_____
_____
_____

What does the word **dilemma** mean? Give an example from Moose's experiences (or your own life) that illustrates this concept.

_____
_____
_____

Vocabulary:

Write a **sentence** using the following words. Make sure that the meaning of the word is clear in your sentence.

inspect – _____
_____

suspicious – _____
_____

criminal – _____
_____

apparent – _____
_____

Al Capone Does My Shirts
by Gennifer Choldenko

economics – _____

relieved – _____

divvying – _____

Questions:

1. In Chapter 16, what does Moose mean when he says that, "Piper is quite the criminal"?

2. What do you think Mr. Trixle means when he says to Piper, "just like your old man"?

3. How did Moose become an accomplice in Piper's project?

4. What main objection did the other students raise when they got their laundry back?

5. Why would it have been better if Moose had told his mom about switching days for baseball right away, instead of waiting until after school the next day?

Al Capone Does My Shirts
by Gennifer Choldenko

6. Both Moose and his mother are in a dilemma. Do you think his mother's solution was fair? What other alternatives can you think of for this situation?
   _____
   _____
   _____

7. a) How did Scout respond to Moose telling him that he couldn't play ball on Tuesday after all?
   _____
   _____

   b) Most conflicts or disagreements have two sides to the story. Explain the point of view of both Moose and Scout in this misunderstanding.

   Moose: _____
   _____

   Scout: _____
   _____

Language Activities:

Conflict is an important element in a novel. There are generally three types of conflict: **person against person**; **person against self**; and **person against nature**. Find examples of conflict in *Al Capone Does My Shirts*, illustrating the first two types.

1. Person against person: _____
   _____
   _____
   _____

2. Person against self: _____
   _____
   _____
   _____

Al Capone Does My Shirts

by Gennifer Choldenko

Chapters 19 – 20

Before you read the chapters:

Has someone ever tried to talk you into doing something that you knew was wrong, or that you really weren't interested in being a part of?
_____
_____

What pressures did you feel in this situation?
_____
_____

What was your final decision, and what important factors helped you make this decision?
_____
_____

Vocabulary:

Choose a word from the list to complete each sentence.

| respectively | distinguished | shenanigans | preposterous | indignity |
| motivated | culpability | monitor | notorious | apparent |

1. Something which is quite obvious is said to be _____.

2. Al Capone was a _____ gangster of the 1930s.

3. "I thought his excuse was quite _____," she said.

4. The final _____ he suffered was losing his hair piece in the wind storm.

5. I hope you will _____ your daughter's actions more closely.

6. If someone is _____ then they are usually recognized as being quite important by society.

Al Capone Does My Shirts
by Gennifer Choldenko

7. I knew that his wise cracks and _____ would eventually get him into trouble.

8. If you are innocent, then your _____ will not be brought into question by the police.

9. The warden questioned Piper and each of the young people _____.

10. The prosecutor claimed that Machine Gun Kelly was _____ by greed.

Questions:

1. After Moose's altercation with Scout, his strategy seems to be to avoid Scout and keep to himself. What other strategy might he have used to help himself get through this difficult time?

   _____
   _____

2. a) How did Piper try to include Natalie in Chapter 19?

   _____
   _____

   b) Why do you think she did this?

   _____
   _____

3. What impression do you have of Mrs. Del S. Peabody III after reading her letter to the warden?

   _____
   _____

4. a) How was the warden unfair in his handling of this situation?

   _____
   _____

Al Capone Does My Shirts
by Gennifer Choldenko

b) What possibly motivated Piper to behave in the way that she did during their interview with the warden?
_____
_____

5. What did Moose do in Chapter 20 that really upset Natalie?
_____
_____

6. **a)** Why didn't Moose get to tell his father first about his meeting with the warden?
_____
_____

b) Why do you think this factor upset his father so much?
_____
_____

Language Activities:

1. Moose's life certainly became a lot more interesting with his move to Alcatraz. Pretend that you are Moose and are writing a letter to your buddy, Pete, back in Santa Monica. Describe for Pete your adventures on the island, some of the people you have met, and how you feel about how your life has changed.

_____
_____
_____
_____
_____
_____
_____
_____

Al Capone Does My Shirts

by Gennifer Choldenko

2. Choose any two characters you've already met in this novel. In the Venn diagram, compare at least four things about these two people. Consider such things as physical appearance, personality, age, talents, attitude, etc.

Character 1:_____   Character 2: _____

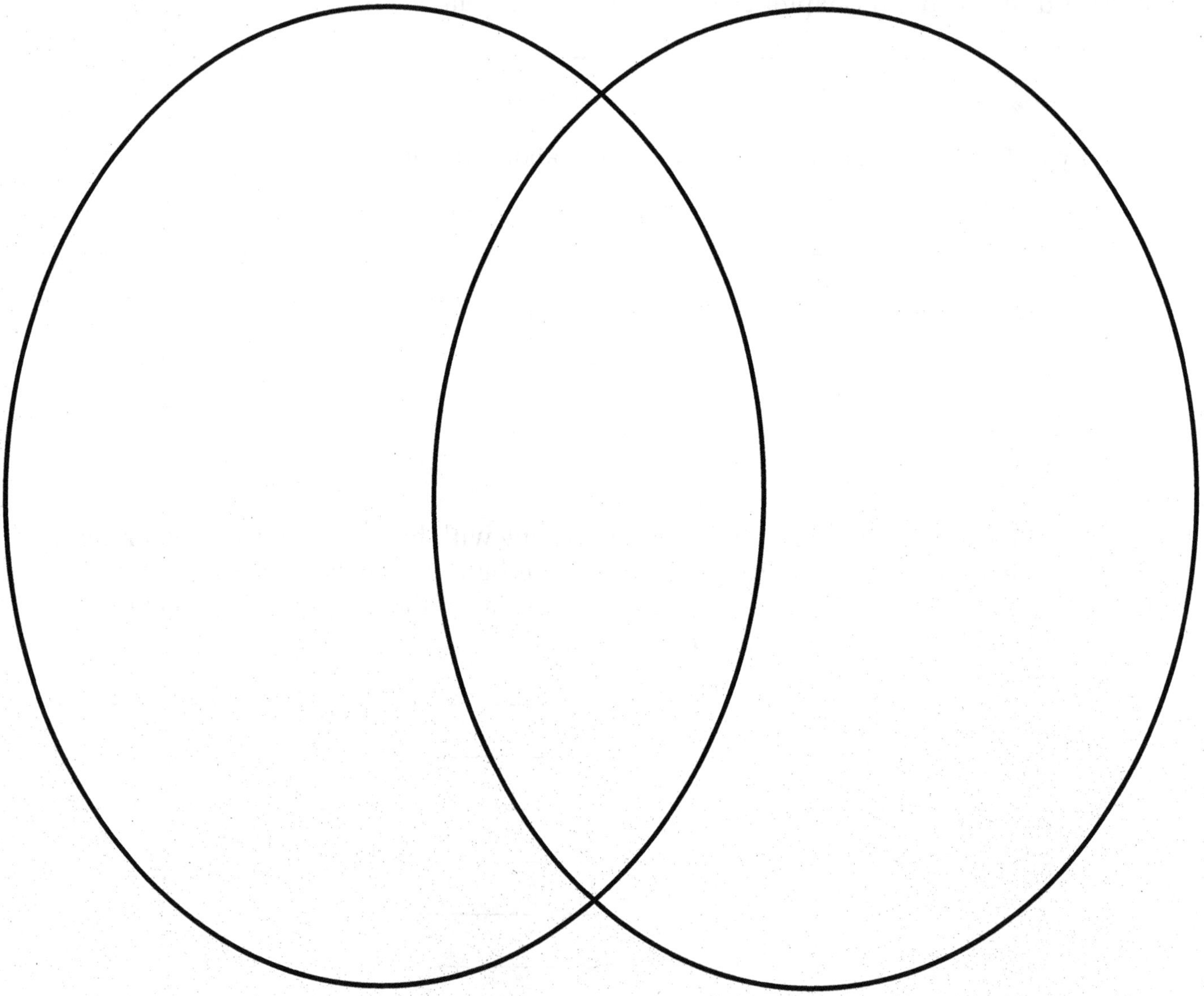

Al Capone Does My Shirts
by Gennifer Choldenko

Chapters 21 – 23

Before you read the chapters:

"The jealous are troublesome to others, but a torment to themselves." ~William Penn

In these chapters Moose experiences the torments of jealousy. What are some things that make people jealous?

_____
_____

Describe a situation in your own life (or that of someone you know) when jealousy was a factor.

_____
_____

Vocabulary:

Synonyms are words with **similar meanings**. Using the context of the sentences below, choose the best synonym or meaning for the underlined words in each sentence.

1. The actor was very **embarrassed** when his pants ripped.
    a) humiliated   b) angry   c) grief-stricken   d) tongue-tied

2. When it came to his baseball glove, Moose was very **possessive**.
    a) imaginative   b) generous   c) selfish   d) determined

3. The expensive medication was not very **effective** in preventing the common cold.
    a) efficient   b) inexpensive   c) calloused   d) complete

4. "I'm afraid you will need an **escort** to enter the building," he said.
    a) ticket   b) attendant   c) letter of permission   d) waif

5. The woodsman **encountered** a wolf down by the lake.
    a) killed   b) trapped   c) played with   d) met

Al Capone Does My Shirts
by Gennifer Choldenko

6. The puzzle looked very **complicated**.

   a) colorful b) expensive c) difficult d) tragic

7. I noticed that my father's neck was **craned** through the performance.

   a) strained b) red c) bruised d) noticeable

8. There was no doubt that the coat was made of **imitation** sealskin.

   a) extensive b) fake c) inexpensive d) damaged

Questions:

1. What did you think of Moose's mom's comment, "don't let Moose fool you, he's smarter than he looks"? How did Moose interpret her comments?
   _____
   _____

2. Why do you think that Moose found Natalie "easier and more present" in recent days?
   _____
   _____

3. Do you think that it was wise for Moose to agree to go on the boat trip to meet Mrs. Capone? Explain your answer.
   _____
   _____

4. What happened to Mrs. Capone when she arrived at Alcatraz?
   _____
   _____

5. Why does Moose want one of the baseballs from Alcatraz?
   _____
   _____

6. How do you know that Moose is a little jealous of Scout's friendship with Piper?
   _____
   _____

Al Capone Does My Shirts

by Gennifer Choldenko

7. What does Natalie do in Chapter 23 that Moose finds very encouraging?

8. Why do you think Moose doesn't want Piper to find a ball for Scout?

Language Activities:

1. The author has a very imaginative way of expressing herself. Rewrite the following sentences from these chapters in your own words:

   "His cries are loud enough to make dogs go deaf."

   "That baby is crying so loudly, Mrs. Mattaman can probably hear him on Alcatraz."

2. Chapter 23 features an example of **personification** (writing about **inanimate objects as if they were a person**, e.g., talking animals or trees). " **the bay is trying very hard to be an ocean**"

   Come up with your own sentences to show personification using the following:

   The wind in an old oak tree late at night.

   A tortoise crossing a highway

Al Capone Does My Shirts

by Gennifer Choldenko

Chapters 24 – 26

Before you read the chapters:

Responsibilities can be overwhelming sometimes for anyone. How much responsibility do you think a person your age should be given by their parents? Think in terms of time, and actual tasks. Please support your views with reasons.

_____
_____
_____
_____
_____

Vocabulary:

Antonyms are words with **opposite meanings**. Draw a line from each word in column A to its antonym in column B. Then use the words in column A to fill in the blanks in the sentences below.

Column A	Column B
scratchy	careless
helter-skelter	unpredictable
regular	normal
incredible	organized
motion	stillness
diligent	smooth
verge	distant

1. My sister has such an _____ singing voice, she recently signed a recording contract.

2. Fireflies at night seem like they are always in _____.

Al Capone Does My Shirts
by Gennifer Choldenko

3. I was on the _____ of losing my temper.

4. In order to succeed in this classroom, you must be a most _____ student.

5. My new wool coast feels _____ against my skin.

6. The little rabbits ran _____ all over the garden.

7. He purchased _____ gasoline at the pumps.

Questions:

Indicate whether the following statements are **True** or **False**.

1. Moose had difficulty squeezing under the fence because of his broad shoulders. T or F

2. What Moose thought was a ball turned out to be a seagull feather. T or F

3. When Moose returned from looking for the ball in Chapter 24, Natalie said, "105". T or F

4. Moose's mom finally started to dress Natalie like her age. T or F

5. Annie got a "convict ball" from the warden. T or F

6. The birds on Alcatraz seemed attracted to Natalie. T or F

7. At the beginning of Chapter 26, Moose finds Natalie sitting with a con. T or F

8. Moose was given a baseball by Machine Gun Kelly. T or F

9. Moose thought it was wonderful that Natalie was spending time with 105. T or F

10. On his last day of searching, Moose found three baseballs. T or F

Al Capone Does My Shirts

by Gennifer Choldenko

Language Activities:

1. Find three examples of the following parts of speech from this chapter.

Nouns	Verbs	Adjectives
_____	_____	_____
_____	_____	_____
_____	_____	_____

2. **Interview** at least three other students for their views of this novel. (Try to get both positive and negative comments.) On a separate sheet of paper, write a brief **report** putting these views together.

3. a) Chapter 25 ends with a real cliffhanger. Describe what is meant by this.

   b) Why is this a popular device used by novelists?

Al Capone Does My Shirts

by Gennifer Choldenko

Chapters 27 – 29

Before you read the chapters:

Moose has a difficult time living with himself in these chapters. Why do you think regret is such a powerful emotion?
_____
_____

What purpose or usefulness do you think regret serves in our lives?
_____
_____

How can regrets be harmful?
_____
_____

Vocabulary:

Analogies are equations in which the **first pair of words has the same relationship as the second pair of words.** For example, **stop** is to **go** as **fast** is to **slow**. In this example, both pairs of words are opposites. Choose the best word from the word box to complete each of the analogies below.

| unreasonable | disloyal | mute | restrain | deficiency |
| balk | typical | disgusted | keen | extraordinary |

1. **Frustrate** is to _____ as **comfortable** is to **content**.

2. **Zealous** is to _____ as **intelligent** is to **smart**.

3. **Encourage** is to _____ as **rough** is to **smooth**.

4. **Blond** is to **dark-haired** as _____ is to **usual**.

5. **Lack** is to _____ as **greedy** is to **covetous**.

Al Capone Does My Shirts
by Gennifer Choldenko

6. **Talkative** is to _____ as **clumsy** is to **agile**.

7. **Deep** is to **shallow** as **unusual** is to _____.

8. **Steadfast** is to **dependable** as **revolted** is to _____.

9. **Cowardice** is to **courage** as _____ is to **patriotic**.

10. **Ludicrous** is to _____ as **beautiful** is to **gorgeous**.

Questions:

1. Explain why you think the author gave Chapter 27 such a harsh title?

2. How do you think the con knew Moose's name?

3. Why did Moose think the con gave him the ball?

4. Why did Piper think it unusual that Moose was "chewing out Natalie"?

5. Why do you think Moose gave Piper the ball after he had spent so long looking for one?

6. What does it probably tell you that at the end of Chapter 26 Natalie mentioned number 105?

Al Capone Does My Shirts
by Gennifer Choldenko

7. Why was Moose's mother so excited in Chapter 28?

8. Give one proof to show that Moose's mother is not completely rational when it comes to Natalie's upbringing.

9. Describe Piper's scheme that she thinks will reveal what is going on between 105 and Natalie?

10. Why was con 105 given so much freedom?

Language Activities:

1. **Sarcasm** is defined as **a cutting remark which makes its victim the butt of ridicule**. Find an example of sarcasm used by Moose in Chapter 29.

2. Copy out any three sentences from this chapter and underline the **verbs**.

Al Capone Does My Shirts
by Gennifer Choldenko

Chapters 30 – 32

Before you read the chapters:

Conflict between two people, no matter what the issue, is often very difficult to resolve. Think of a time when you experienced conflict in your life (either directly or as a witness). Describe the circumstances, the issues, and how it eventually was resolved (if it was).

_____
_____
_____
_____
_____

Vocabulary:

Circle the correct meaning for each underlined word.

1. The soldiers were able to **repel** the attack.

    a) photograph b) escape c) ward off d) laugh at

2. Not one **critical** word comes out of her mouth.

    a) unfavorable b) loving c) abstract d) intelligent

3. The situation with Natalie and con 105 was very **complicated**.

    a) expensive b) deceptive c) playful d) intricate

4. Natalie looked very **forlorn** as she lay on the red carpet.

    a) happy b) sad c) angry d) triumphant

5. Her hands and feet were **flailing** on the floor.

    a) soaking wet b) bleeding c) thrashing d) tied together

6. Piper thought that the attitude of Moose's mother was **ridiculous**.

    a) silly b) criminal c) promising d) improving

Al Capone Does My Shirts
by Gennifer Choldenko

7. The fans were all **riveted** to the spectacular play unfolding before them.
   a) outraged b) concentrating on c) complaining about d) looking for

8. Do you think that Moose **respects** his father?
   a) works for b) loves c) abhors d) esteems

9. Theresa walked up the **incline** to the boat.
   a) ramp b) dock c) gangplank d) pathway

10. Natalie threw one of her **tantrums**.
    a) stuffed animal b) crayons c) temper fits d) kettle drums

Questions:

1. a) At the beginning of Chapter 30, why did Moose long to tell his mother about Natalie and con 105?

   b) What kept Moose from acting on this?

2. a) Why do you think Moose's mom took Natalie's buttons with her?

   b) Do you think it was fair for her to take these buttons? Explain your answer.

3. Moose basically accuses his dad of being hen-pecked. Do you agree? Support your answer with proof from the novel.

Al Capone Does My Shirts

by Gennifer Choldenko

4. Reread the closing paragraph in Chapter 31. Why do you think Moose would be relieved at his father's answer in this paragraph?
   _____
   _____

5. Why do you think Moose's dad finally took a stand in Chapter 32?
   _____
   _____

Language Activities:

1. Imagine that you are a newspaper editor for San Francisco Chronicle back in the 1930s and you are writing an **editorial** on the topic of Alcatraz Prison. Introduce your readers to the fact that there are children living on this notorious island. An editorial usually expresses a strong point of view on a topic. Your point of view might be: Alcatraz is an unsafe place for children to live; or Alcatraz is a fascinating place for children to live; or another point of view of your choosing.

   July 13, 1930

   Dear Editor, _____
   _____
   _____
   _____
   _____
   _____
   _____
   _____
   _____
   _____

   Yours truly, _____

Al Capone Does My Shirts
by Gennifer Choldenko

2. Create and design a **wanted poster** advertising a reward for the capture of one of the famous gangsters of the 1930s. Your poster should include a sketch of the fugitive; pertinent information about him; the amount of the reward; and who should be contacted if this person is spotted.

Al Capone Does My Shirts
by Gennifer Choldenko

Chapters 33 – 34

Before you read the chapters:

Think about a time when you were really looking forward to something. Describe what it was you were looking forward to and exactly how you felt.

_____
_____
_____

Was what you were looking forward to worth the wait and excitement?

_____
_____
_____

Vocabulary:

In each of the following sets of words, underline the one word that does not belong. Then write a sentence explaining why it does not fit.

1. celebration   festivity   gala   pompadour

   _____

2. considerable   great   ordinance   powerful

   _____

3. talented   obsessed   fascinated   consumed

   _____

4. pretend   discern   imagine   feign

   _____

5. sincere   offense   discourtesy   umbrage

   _____

Al Capone Does My Shirts

by Gennifer Choldenko

6. earnest	serious	solemn	talkative

_____

7. vulnerable	weak	comical	tender

_____

8. sloping	abrupt	sharp	unexpected

_____

Questions:

1. **a)** After you have read Chapter 33, comment on why the author gave it the title, *The Sun and the Moon*.

   _____
   _____

   b) Suggest another title for this chapter.

   _____
   _____

2. **a)** What did Moose's mother admit that Moose was better at than her?

   _____

   b) Why do you think Moose was better at it?

   _____
   _____

3. Why didn't Moose want to let Piper into the house?

   _____
   _____

4. What was the underlying reason for Natalie being so upset in Chapter 33?

   _____
   _____

Al Capone Does My Shirts
by Gennifer Choldenko

5. a) The author includes a brief description of con 105 near the end of Chapter 33. In point form, list the four items of description she includes.

   _____   _____
   _____   _____

   b) What impression of this man are you left with?

   _____
   _____

6. Who came to Natalie's birthday party?

   _____
   _____

Language Activities:

1. The last sentence in Chapter 34 features a literary device known as **foreshadowing** (**to suggest beforehand or to hint as to what is about to happen**). Why might it be significant that Piper used the word we, when telling Moose, "That's what we figured"? What might this mean about what Moose's friends have been discussing behind his back?

   _____
   _____
   _____

2. With a straight line, match each character from *Al Capone Does My Shirts* with a quotation made by that character. (These quotations go back to the beginning of the novel.)

   a) Theresa   1. "Cover your ears, young lady."
   b) Con 105   2. "They teach you how to be a nice little church boy in Santa Monica?"
   c) Miss Bimp   3. "Take it easy, fella. I got your baseball, didn't I?"
   d) The Warden   4. "If it's more than ten days overdue, they put you in the hole."
   e) Piper   5. "First we're going to the morgue."
   f) Scout   6. "You get a convict baseball you'll show it to me first, right?"
   g) Moose   7. "Are you certain you have the right class?"

Al Capone Does My Shirts
by Gennifer Choldenko

Chapters 35 – 37

Before you read the chapters:

"The worst lies are the lies we tell ourselves. We do this because we're afraid." ~ Richard Bach

The lies that Moose's mother told about Natalie eventually came back to haunt her. Why is **lying** a bad habit to get into? Do you think it is ever right to tell a lie? Explain your answer.

_____
_____
_____
_____
_____

Vocabulary:

Draw a straight line to connect the vocabulary word to its definition. Remember to use a straight edge (like a ruler).

1. quiver
2. institution
3. radiant
4. uncomfortable
5. instinct
6. seething
7. understate
8. aluminum
9. precedent
10. mockery

a) distressed
b) a metal
c) glowing
d) laughingstock
e) misrepresent
f) tremble
g) example
h) raging
i) asylum
j) intuition

Al Capone Does My Shirts

by Gennifer Choldenko

Questions:

1. Why does Moose decide to make Natalie's age a huge issue in Chapter 35?

2. What was his mother's reasoning in wishing to keep Natalie at ten years old?

3. What did Natalie do at the interview with Mr. Purdy that her mother considered a real breakthrough?

4. What does the following statement by Moose about his mother in Chapter 36 tell you about their relationship? "She never tries to imagine how I feel."

5. What devastating news does the family receive at the end of Chapter 36?

6. What was Mrs. Kelly's reaction to Mr. Purdy's decision?

7. What surprising solution to the problem does Moose suggest to the warden?

8. What reason does the warden give for rejecting this suggestion?

Al Capone Does My Shirts

by Gennifer Choldenko

Language Activities:

1. The author uses many **similes** in this novel. Here are a few from previous chapters:

   a) "flipping a flat yellow hat on her finger like a pizza"

   b) "my ears are like two heaters attached to my head"

   c) "the ball, my glove, my arm are all working together like greased motor parts"

   d) "with arms as big as thighs"

   e) "Natalie has stacks of buttons... like little soldiers guarding something"

   Complete the following chart, indicating what two things are being compared in each simile. The first one is done for you:

	Item #1	Item #2
a)	flat yellow hat	pizza
b)		
c)		
d)		
e)		

2. Try to reassemble the word parts listed below into ten compound words, which are found in this chapter.

six	up	body	picks	in	to	step	teen	fast	every
statement	work	make	side	day	under	tooth	break	stool	home

   1. _____
   2. _____
   3. _____
   4. _____
   5. _____
   6. _____
   7. _____
   8. _____
   9. _____
   10. _____

Al Capone Does My Shirts
by Gennifer Choldenko

Chapters 38 – 40

Before you read the chapters:

Have you ever read a book before that had a surprise ending?
_____

What would be the advantage to reading (or writing) a novel with a surprise ending?
_____
_____

Vocabulary:

Use a dictionary to find the meanings of the following words:

shredded – _____
_____

quiver – _____
_____

gritty – _____
_____

duplicate – _____
_____

grateful – _____
_____

spontaneous – _____
_____

Al Capone Does My Shirts
by Gennifer Choldenko

apparent – _____

launch – _____

haste – _____

Questions:

1. Describe two immediate effects on Moose's parents that result from Natalie being rejected from the Esther P. Marinoff School.

2. Who did Natalie think her mother was mad at?

3. How was Moose able to get a letter to Al Capone through to him?

4. a) How did Piper save face after being sent to stay with her grandmother?

   b) Was this punishment effective? Explain your answer.

Al Capone Does My Shirts

by Gennifer Choldenko

5. Why do you think Moose insisted on keeping the last sentence of his letter?

6. Reread the last paragraph of Chapter 38. What do you think this means in terms of Piper's relationship with Moose?

7. Why did Moose think moving back to Santa Monica would be bad for Natalie?

8. What do you think is meant by Moose's dad's expression, "Nobody knows until they go ahead and play the game"?

9. Do you think this was an effective conclusion to this novel? Defend your answer.

Language Activities:

1. On a separate sheet, create a time line for *Al Capone Does My Shirts* indicating the 10 most important events of the novel and the order in which they happened. The author is helpful in that she includes the date with each chapter title.

2. On a separate sheet, create a book cover for *Al Capone Does My Shirts*. Be sure to include the title, author, and a picture that will make other students want to read the novel.

Answer Key

Chapters 1 – 2: *(page 10)*

Vocabulary:
1. embezzler
2. picky
3. apparent
4. smithereens
5. buoy
6. stilts
7. felon
8. circuits
9. affliction
10. tantrum

Questions:
1. a) Answers may vary (e.g., Why is he living on Alcatraz Island?).
   b) It was very bleak – covered with cement and bird turd.
   c) It begins on January 4, 1935.
2. Their dad got a job as an electrician in the prison.
3. Answers may vary (e.g., the students must have been quite unusual there).
4. For fear of being disarmed by the prisoners.
5. She is small for her age, she doesn't communicate very fluently. She is probably autistic.
6. Answers may vary (e.g., He probably liked the name and tailored his personality to fit the image).
7. He slept with his shoes on and had a baseball bat with him in bed. This was probably not necessary, but it would make him feel safer.
8. Theresa has black curly hair and is missing half her teeth. She is quite a bit younger than Moose and is very outspoken and opinionated.

Language Activities:
2. simile – water is compared to tar
3. Answers may vary (e.g., kids have macaroni salad in their hair; she can take one look at her box and name the exact button I have).
4. Answers may vary (e.g., dear, honey, big guy).

Chapters 3 – 4: *(page 14)*

Vocabulary:

[Crossword puzzle with answers: CAPONE, PRONOUNCE, SWIPE, CLEAT, SASE, REALIZE, RESUME, ACHES, SUDDENLY, AUTISTIC, SNITCH, etc.]

Questions:
1. Dead criminal checker
2. Jimmy and eleven little boys
3. a) Scarface, Big Al, Snorkey
   b) Answers may vary depending on the year question is asked (he was born in 1899).
4. A person forgets important details about a crime when threatened.
5. They were dead.
6. Answers may vary (e.g., Probably because he feels very protective of her and perhaps embarrassed).
7. She is very good with numbers and calculations.
8. He wonders whether his parents have told the warden about Natalie's condition.
9. Answers may vary (e.g., it is hard to fake a genuine smile).
10. A metal detector
11. Moose could tell that Natalie felt very frightened (she held his hand for the first time).

Language Activities:
1. Answers may vary. For example: Autism: Challenges with: social interactions; verbal and non-verbal communication; the ability to learn (in the usual settings); repetitive behaviors; unusual or severely limited activities and interests.

2. Answers may vary. For example: American Leaf-Nosed Bat: small to medium sized; they have a visible tail that ranges from 1.4 to 1.6 inches; have a large noseleaf, large ears, and broad wings; their fur is brown or gray; the underside is lighter, typically a brown or tan color; only a few species of this family found in the United States; live in extremely dry habitats; they roost in caves, mines, and abandoned buildings; eat insects, such as crickets, moths, beetles
3. a) to hurry   b) the boat trip is only 12 minutes long, but some prison terms are 20 years
    c) Natalie is often not aware of people or her surroundings.

Chapters 5 – 6: *(page 18)*
Vocabulary:
1. obsession – the other words are all health care facilities
2. pail – a homonym of pale, which is a synonym of the other two words meaning discolored
3. cowardly – the other words all mean to act kindly toward
4. ferocious – the other words are all synonyms of impressive.
5. menacing – the other words all mean quiet
6. deliberate – the other words all mean ghastly
7. grossly – the other words all deal with the concept of accuracy

Questions:

   Mrs. McCraw offended Moose's mom by saying that Natalie belonged in an **asylum**. When they returned home from taking Natalie to her school, there was a note asking that Moose see the **warden** later that afternoon. Moose thought that being a prison **guard** was the wrong job for his dad. Moose learned at an early age that getting mad at **Natalie** would never be forgiven. Moose's dad said about **Piper** that "the pretty ones are always trouble". Moose's dad said that the **convicts** darned socks a lot better than his mom.

   Moose met the warden in the **library**. The warden told him that everyone on Alcatraz must follow the rules without **exception**. The warden reminded Moose that the convicts were **terrible** men with nothing but **time** on their hands. The warden thought it important that he and Moose **understand** each other. Rule number one: There's no **contact** with the convicts. Rule number four: Do not speak to **outsiders** about what goes on here. He said that the point of the prison is to keep showy criminals out of the **limelight**. Finally, the warden asked Moose if would mind helping Piper carry her **projects** to school.

Language Activities:
1. Answers may vary.   2. Answers may vary (e.g., cin/na/mon).

Chapters 7 – 9: *(page 21)*
Vocabulary:
1. c   2. j   3. b   4. h   5. e   6. a   7. g   8. d   9. f   10. i

Questions:
1. He regards her as a piece of work and an enemy.
2. Answers may vary (e.g., Moose probably has too much responsibility for his age).
3. Answers may vary (e.g., she seems very uptight).
4. Piper probably feels she is special and above the rules.
5. To impress the other students
6. Answers may vary (e.g., the most exciting thing that happened to me this vacation . . . dad brought home a plate of roast chicken).
7. He hit a liner to short and reached first base due to a bad throw.
8. Answers may vary (e.g., he could forget his responsibilities; he was a good athlete and would be admired for this).
9. Moose won't help Piper with her "project".
10. Moose asks her if she saw him play ball after school, and then is embarrassed for asking.

Language Activities:
1. Answers may vary.
2. selves, speeches, women, contraptions, catches, cries, halves, churches, laundries, notebooks

Chapters 10 – 12: *(page 24)*
Vocabulary:
1. flexibility   2. register   3. radiant   4. sensitive   5. diagnosis   6. formula
7. adjustment   8. replicate   9. swiveled   10. permanent

Questions:
1. That Natalie was not settling in at the school.
2. He knows that his mom won't take the news well, and that his dad can deliver the news to her.
3. She probably hopes to convince Mr. Purdy to keep Natalie and feels she has a better chance of convincing him without her husband at the meeting.
4. University of California, Los Angeles campus.
5. They did not treat her respectfully, as a person.
6. The program had a successful reputation with autistic children.
7. Heat treatments; aluminum formula
8. Natalie screamed for over an hour early in the morning.
9. Answers may vary.
10. Convicts who think they know as much about the law as their lawyers do.
11. She promises to be nice to Natalie.

Language Activities:
1. Answers may vary (e.g., arms as big as thighs; bosoms like two jiggly watermelons; the cabin, where it's warm and steamy like hot chocolate).
3. Caconi, can, cereal, child, children, classroom, come, country, cracks, creases

Chapters 13 – 15: *(page 27)*
Vocabulary:

```
c a p o n e q w e e l d d u h
e o r t y u i o o p a s d f p
f g r h j y l l e v a r g r e
z x n d c v b n m q w e e v n
q w a e u r t y u i o c r i t
r q t s d r f g h j i r j c e
e a t s c a o s d o f e h t r
d z e z x u y y u t r v e o t
i x r c v b n s s m q v w r a
r e s p o n s i b i l i t y i
e p o u y t r e w q w n d f n
c s d f e l d e e h w g h j
t s r e c r e a t i o n f g h
```

Questions:
1. That Natalie should have some sessions with Carrie Kelly, and if she shows improvement, then she will be readmitted to the school.
2. He tells her that she is lucky that Moose caught her going through the laundry and not one of his parents.
3. Answers may vary (e.g., she is a trained professional, so even though her measures seem harsh, they might be good for Natalie's progress socially).
4. She wants him to look after Natalie each day after school. It is a problem because Moose plays ball one of those days.
5. Because Moose's mom is such a determined person.
6. The talk went quite well, although Moose sort-of promised Scout a "convict baseball".
7. Her practical mind told her that it was a hot day, Moose was wearing a bathing suit, so why couldn't she wear one?
8. Answers may vary (e.g., probably took it from her dad's key ring).

Language Activities:
1. Answes may vary.
2. a) It was Tuesday before Moose even got to leave Alcatraz.
   b) Don't you really care what happened to Natalie?
   c) Piper spotted Al Capone doing laundry at the Shady Rest Hotel.
3. Answers may vary (e.g., screech, thud, ka-pow).

Chapters 16 – 18: *(page 30)*
Before You Read:
dilemma: a problem that seems to defy a satisfactory solution

Vocabulary:
Answers may vary.

Questions:
1. Piper was able to get the extra laundry out of Moose's family's laundry bags without them knowing.

2. She had an answer for everything. (She was a smooth-talker.)
3. By helping her carry the laundry.
4. There was nothing special about the way they looked - other than the fact that they were clean.
5. She might have been able to make allowances for this in her schedule.
6. Answers may vary (e.g., she might have made an exception).
7. a) Scout is very upset. Tells Moose he won't be playing on his team again.
   b) Answers may vary (e.g., Moose has to look after his sister – his family is counting on him. Scout has changed the time of the ball game for Moose, and now Moose has changed his mind).

Language Activities:
Person – person: Piper - Moose; Moose – Scout; Moose – his mother; Moose – Natalie
Person – Self: Moose and himself (i.e., his responsibilities are getting to be too much for him)

Chapters 19 – 20: *(page 33)*
Vocabulary:
1. apparent   2. notorious   3. preposterous   4. indignity   5. monitor
6. distinguished   7. shenanigans   8. culpability   9. respectively   10. motivated

Questions:
1. Answers may vary (e.g., he could have tried to explain things to Scout).
   a) By getting her to count the money
   b) Answers may vary (e.g., Perhaps she is trying to get on Moose's good side because she likes him).
2. She seems very shrill and bossy.
3. a) He didn't give anyone a chance to speak to the situation, and punished them all equally.
   b) Answers may vary (e.g., fear).
4. He upset Natalie's button box.
5. a) Because of the crisis with Natalie being upset.
   b) He didn't think he could trust Moose.

Language Activities:
Answers may vary.

Chapters 21 – 23: *(page 37)*
Vocabulary:
1. a   2. c   3. a   4. b   5. d   6. c   7. a   8. b

Questions:
1. Answers may vary (e.g., Even my own mother thinks I look stupid).
2. Answers may vary (e.g., because of Mrs. Kelly's classes).
3. Answers may vary (e.g., It might jeopardize his father's job if the incident upsets the warden).
4. The metal detector indicated that she had metal in her clothing. She was subjected to a strip search and returned to San Francisco in humiliation on the next boat.
5. to give to Scout
6. He is upset that they talk together in French class.
7. She tries to imitate Mrs. Kelly.
8. It will enhance their friendship.

Language Activities:
Answers may vary.

Chapters 24 – 26: *(page 40)*
Vocabulary:
incredible-normal; motion-stillness; verge-distant; diligent-careless; scratchy-smooth; helter-skelter-organized; regular-unpredictable
1. incredible   2. motion   3. verge   4. diligent   5. scratchy   6. helter-skelter   7. regular

Questions:
1. T   2. F   3. T   4. F   5. F   6. T   7. T   8. F   9. F   10. F

Language Activities:
1. Answers may vary. For example: *Nouns:* bushes, shirt, tooth   *Verbs:* spin, run, wearing
   Adjectives: denim, dark, rare
3. Answers may vary (e.g., Cliffhanger: left in the middle of some action, not knowing what will happen next. Novelists use it because it builds suspense and curiosity in the reader).

Chapters 27 – 29: *(page 43)*
Vocabulary:
1. balk 2. keen 3. restrain 4. extraordinary 5. deficiency
6. mute 7. typical 8. disgusted 9. disloyal 10. unreasonable

Questions:
1. It shows the intensity of Moose's feelings about the situation.
2. Small island. Words gets around among the cons – especially one with the freedom that this con enjoyed.
3. Insurance; he figured he could buy Moose off.
4. Because he never raised his voice to her.
5. Answers may vary (e.g., he felt guilty about leaving Natalie alone, and the ball was a reminder of that).
6. He had made an indelible impression on her.
7. A newspaper had reported on breakthroughs at the Esther P. Marinoff school.
8. Answers may vary (e.g., she lied about Natalie's age).
9. They will use Natalie as bait, then hide and watch them.
10. He was close to his release date.

Language Activities:
Sarcasm: "I mean, dropping your purse on her toe. Nice touch."

Chapters 30 – 32: *(page 46)*
Vocabulary:
1. c 2. a 3. d 4. b 5. c 6. a 7. b 8. d 9. a 10. c

Questions:
1. a) Answers may vary (e.g., guilt).
   b) Answers may vary (e.g., He knows his mother is an emotional wreck and will take it very badly).
2. a) Mrs. Kelly had suggested it.
   b) Answers may vary (e.g., No, because it left Moose to bear the brunt of the results).
3. Answers may vary (e.g., He does seem to bend to his wife's wishes most of the time).
4. He absolved Moose of all blame for causing Natalie's condition.
5. He knew that Moose was right, and was speaking his mind for Natalie's benefit.

Chapters 33 – 34: *(page 50)*
Vocabulary:
1. pompadour – the other words involve a celebration
2. ordinance – the other words involve greatness
3. talented – the other words deal with talent
4. discern – the other words deal with the imagination
5. sincere – the other words involve an act of rudeness
6. talkative – the other words deal with being talkative
7. comical – the other words all involve weakness
8. sloping – the other words all involve something which is abrupt

Questions:
1. a) Answers may vary (e.g., a reference to Natalie's pictures that she is drawing).
   b) Answers may vary.
2. a) He was better with Natalie than she was.
   b) Answers may vary (e.g., Moose was more relaxed around Natalie).
3. He wanted to keep Natalie quiet.
4. She wanted to go out and visit con 105.
5. a) black greased hair; short bulbed nose; pockmarked skin; uneven walk.
   b) Answers may vary (e.g., not very favorable or flattering).
6. Natalie's parents, Natalie, Moose, Theresa, Annie, and Jimmy

Language Activities:
1. Piper's use of the word "we" means that she and the others have been discussing Natalie's age when Moose wasn't around. It is an example of foreshadowing because it indicates that others are probably aware of the fact that Natalie is older than what her parents have been telling people.
2. a) 5. b) 3. c) 7. d) 1. e) 2. f) 6. g) 4.

Chapters 35 – 37: *(page 53)*
Vocabulary:
1. f 2. i 3. c 4. a 5. j 6. h 7. e 8. b 9. g 10. d

Questions:
1. He feels Natalie will never get accepted into the school if they lie about her age.

2. She felt Natalie would have a chance in the world as a child, but not as an adult.
3. She told a joke.
4. He felt that his mother took him for granted and never took his feelings into consideration.
5. Natalie was not accepted into the school.
6. She was disappointed. She felt Natalie would be accepted this time.
7. He suggested that the warden approach Al Capone to see if the gangster might pull a few strings to have Natalie admitted.
8. He was afraid that Capone would expect preferential treatment as a reward.

Language Activities:
1. ears – heaters; ball, glove, arm – greased motor parts; arms – thighs; buttons – soldiers
2. sixteen, everybody, inside, today, stepstool, homework, makeup, understatement, toothpicks, breakfast

Chapters 38 – 40: *(page 56)*

Vocabulary:
Answers may vary.

Questions:
1. Moose's mother stays in her room; his father takes over the cooking.
2. At Natalie
3. Piper smuggled it past her mother (the censor).
4. a) By saying that she loved it.
   b) Probably; her behavior improved.
5. The Mom Rule - makes him act better.
6. She probably likes him.
7. Answers may vary. (e.g., Natalie seems to be adjusting to Alcatraz, and another change would upset her).
8. You'll never know until you try.
9. Answers may vary.